An Illustrated Guide to Mythical Heroes

A gripping introduction to the warriors, kings and monster-slayers found in the myths, legends and folklore of cultures around the world, with illustrations by David West and text by Anita Ganeri.

BOOK HOUSE

An Illustrated Guide to Mythical Heroes
was produced by

David West 🏃🏃 **Children's Books**
7 Princeton Court, 55 Felsham Road, London SW15 1AZ

Designed and illustrated by David West
Written by Anita Ganeri and David West

First published in the UK in MMX *by* Book House,
an imprint of The Salariya Book Company Ltd.,
25, Marlborough Place, Brighton BN1 1UB

SALARIYA

Please visit the Salariya Book Company at:
www.book-house.co.uk

Printed on paper from sustainable forests.

11 10 09 08 07
10 9 8 7 6 5 4 3 2 1

ISBN: 978 1 906714 82 6 (hardback)
ISBN: 978 1 906714 83 3 (paperback)

A CIP catalogue record for this book is available from the British Library.

Printed and bound in China.

Photo Credits:
1,Bibi Saint-Pol; 10b, ONAR; 21r,
Eupator; 36b, Ilussion; 38m, Lars
Henriksson; 42b, Anatoly Terentiev;

Contents

Introduction

Welcome to the dangerous world of myth, where adventurous heroes risk life and limb on perilous quests. Witness noble warriors seeking to gain fame and fortune as they fight each other for the world's most beautiful women. Accompany heroic supermen as they take on evil monsters and enormous giants, and applaud the courage of those who battle and defeat the powers of evil. Read on and prepare to relive the fantastic feats and journeys of mythical heroes from around the world.

The Greek hero, Herakles, takes on the three-bodied giant, Geryon.

Odysseus ties himself to the ship's mast to avoid the lure of the Sirens' voices.

6

Epic Heroes

Heroes figure large in ancient epic tales and poems. Often, it is the task of the hero to be sent on a great quest in search of a person or object, to fulfil the command of a king, or simply to find their way home. Whatever the reasons behind them, our heroes' journeys are always filled with adventures and challenges that must be overcome.

After blinding the Cyclops, Odysseus and his men escape by hanging under the giant's sheep as they are let out of the cave.

The journey of Odysseus

The ancient Greek epic poem, the Odyssey, is thought to have been written by Homer towards the end of the 8th century BC. It tells the astonishing story of the hero, Odysseus, and his turbulent, ten-year journey home at the end of the Trojan War. First, his ships are driven off course by storms and he loses six men from each ship in battle. Then, he calls at the island of the Cyclops, Polyphemus, who shuts the men in a cave with his sheep and starts to eat them, one by one. Later, the survivors visit Aeolus, guardian of the winds. He gives Odysseus a bag containing the storm winds, to ensure a safe passage home. Foolishly, the sailors open the bag while Odysseus is sleeping, thinking it contains gold. The storms they unleash drive the ships back to Aeaea, home to the witch Circe, who turns the men into pigs. Having made their escape, they sail safely past the Sirens, whose singing is known to lure ships to their doom on the rocks. But even then the danger is not over. They must navigate through a narrow channel between two monsters, Scylla and Charibdis. Later, Odysseus is washed up on the island of Ortygia where the goddess, Calypso, keeps him prisoner for seven years. Finally, he reaches Ithaca.

Near Telepylos, Odysseus's ships are attacked by giants who throw rocks and spears at the men in the water (above).

Back home, Odysseus kills all the nobles who tried to persuade his wife, Penelope, to marry them and to give away Odysseus's kingdom (left).

7

After ploughing the field, Jason throws a stone at the army of warriors.

Jason and the Argonauts

Another great Greek hero is Jason, the leader of the Argonauts. Heir to the throne of Iolcus, Jason is banished by his wicked uncle, King Pelias, but returns to claim his rightful crown. Pelias agrees, on condition that Jason fetches the Golden Fleece from Colchis – a seemingly impossible quest. Jason has a great ship, the Argo, built and he assembles a group of heroes, the Argonauts, to accompany him.

The Argonauts visit King Phineas and ask his advice on the dangers ahead. The king agrees to help, but only if they can get rid of the Harpies – terrible, bird-like monsters that screech and steal food so their victims cannot sleep or eat. The Argonauts chase the Harpies out to sea and Phineas tells them how to reach Colchis, by sailing through the Clashing Rocks, huge cliffs that crash shut on ships. Phineas advises them to send a bird through first to make the rocks close. Then, as the rocks reopen, the Argonauts must row with all their might.

At Colchis, King Aetes promises Jason the Golden Fleece if he can complete a series of tasks. First, Jason must plough a field with fire-breathing oxen. Medea, the king's daughter, helps Jason by giving him a potion to protect him from the bulls' breath. Next, he plants some dragons' teeth which sprout into an army of warriors. Medea tells him to throw a stone at the warriors, as this will make them fight amongst themselves. Finally, Jason overcomes the dragon that guards the Golden Fleece by lulling it to sleep. Having seized the Fleece, Jason begins his eventful journey back to Iolcus.

Medea gives Jason a magic potion of herbs (above). Jason uses the potion to lull the dragon guarding the Golden Fleece to sleep (below).

Aeneas and the Aeneads

The son of the goddess Aphrodite (Venus), Aeneas is the hero of the Aeneid, an epic poem written by the Roman poet, Virgil, in the 1st century BC. It tells the story of Aeneas's travels to Italy, at the end of the Trojan War. When Troy falls, Aeneas is one of the few Trojan nobles to survive the slaughter. Commanded by the gods to flee the city, he gathers a group of companions, known as the Aeneads, which includes his son, Ascanius, his father, Anchises, and several of his most trusted friends.

As in many epic journeys, Aeneas's ships are driven off course by storms at sea.

Aeneas tell the story of his voyage to Dido, Queen of Carthage.

After a voyage which lasts for six years, Aeneas and his men eventually land at the city of Carthage on the coast of North Africa. There, Aeneas falls in love with Dido, Queen of Carthage, who wants the Trojans to settle in her lands and to rule jointly with Aeneas. The gods have different ideas, however, and after a year they remind Aeneas that it is time to set off on his travels again. Aeneas leaves the city secretly. When Dido discovers that he has gone, she builds a burning pyre to destroy his possessions then commits suicide. Later, when Aeneas travels to Hades, the land of the dead, he speaks to Dido's spirit but she does not even acknowledge him.

Aeneas fights for Lavinia.

Leaving Carthage, Aeneas sails to Sicily and from there to mainland Italy. Latinus, king of the Latins, welcomes the Aeneads and allows them to settle in his land. Aeneas marries the king's daughter, Lavinia, and, after his death, he is made a god. Legend says that his descendants and those of the other Trojans went on to found the city of Rome. Later, the great Roman leader, Julius Caesar, also traced his ancestry back to Aeneas.

The Twelve Labours of Herakles

One of the greatest heroes of Greek mythology is Herakles. The son of the god, Zeus, and a princess, Alcemene, he is famous for his superhuman strength and courage. Legend says that the goddess, Hera, wife of Zeus, hated Herakles, because of Zeus's affair with Herakles's mother. A few months after Herakles's birth, Hera sends two serpents to kill him as he lay in his cot. Herakles strangles them both, surprising everyone with his great strength. Later, Hera drives Herakles so mad that he kills his wife and children. Horrified at what he has done, he offers his services to King Eurystheus who sets him twelve seemingly impossible tasks. If Herakles can complete them all, he will be rid of his guilt and become immortal.

Herakles kills the Nemean Lion and later wears its skin as protection.

The first of Herakles's twelve labours is to kill the Nemean lion, a terrifying beast with a skin so tough that no weapon can pierce it. The only way that Herakles can slay the lion is to stun it with his club, then strangle it with his bare hands. He returns to King Eurystheus with the lion's pelt which the king gives to him to wear from then on. For his second labour, Herakles must kill the Lernean Hydra (see page 23). His third labour is even more difficult. He must capture the Ceryneian Hind, a mythical deer that is so fast it can outrun an arrow. Herakles pursues the deer on foot and finally catches it in a net.

Capturing the Ceryneian Hind alive is much more difficult than killing it because it can run so fast (below). Herakles has to chase it for a year before he can catch it. The Hind is sacred to Artemis, goddess of hunting and the moon.

Herakles uses his great strength to catch the Cretan Bull, before taking it back to King Eurystheus by boat.

Herakles's fourth labour is to trap the Erymanthian Boar, an enormous and highly dangerous animal from Mount Erymanthos. On his way, Herakles visits the centaur, Chiron, for advice. Chiron tells him to drive the boar into thick snow to make it easier to catch. After Herakles has caught the boar, Eurystheus sets him his fifth labour – to clean the Augean stables in a single day. The stables have never been cleaned before and are piled high with dung. Not even Herakles can complete this task by himself. Instead, he succeeds in diverting the course of two nearby rivers so that they sweep through the stables.

The sixth labour pits Herakles against the Stymphalian birds, ferocious, man-eating birds with bronze beaks, claws and wings. By shouting loudly, he startles the birds so that they fly up into the air, then he shoots them with his arrows. For his seventh labour, Herakles must capture the Cretan Bull, the father of the famous Minotaur. The eighth labour is to round up the Mares of Diomedes. These wild horses eat human flesh and belong to the giant, Diomedes.

For his ninth task, Herakles has to fetch a girdle from Hippolyte, Queen of the Amazons. Intrigued by Herakles's lion skin and strength, Hippolyte gives him the girdle without a fight. Next, he travels to the island of Erytheia to fetch the Cattle of Geryon. But first, he must kill the two-headed guard dog, Orthrus, and Geryon himself, a three-bodied giant (see pages 4-5). The eleventh labour is to steal the Golden Apples of the Hesperides belonging to the goddess Hera. Herakles tricks the giant, Atlas, into stealing the apples for him by offering to take the weight of the heavens for a while. For his final labour, Herakles must capture Cerberus, the three-headed dog that guards the gates of the Underworld.

Some versions of the legend tell how Herakles was helped by a group of youths to round up the Mares of Diomedes (above). Using his bare hands, Herakles kills Diomedes and feeds him to the mares. This makes them calmer and easier to catch.

Having caught the Erymanthian Boar, Herakles takes it back to Eurystheus. The king is so frightened that he tries to hide in a large, storage jar.

The sculptor of the statue below clearly made a mistake on his depiction of Herakles' final task. Hades, god of the dead, gives Herakles permission to take Cerberus if Herakles can overpower the dog without using weapons. Herakles manages to do so and drags the beast all the way back to Eurystheus's court.

Orpheus

Legend says that Orpheus was the best musician in Ancient Greece, and that his music had magical powers. As one of the Argonauts (see page 8), Orpheus uses his skills to save his companions. On their homeward voyage, the Argonauts pass the Sirens (see page 6). When Orpheus hears them, he takes out his lyre and plays loud and beautiful music to drown out the bewitching sound of their voices. Later, Orpheus marries the goddess, Eurydice, but she dies of a snake-bite. Heartbroken, Orpheus follows her to the Underworld and begs Hades to let her go. Hades is charmed by Orpheus's music and agrees, on condition that Orpheus lead Eurydice away without looking at her. But Orpheus cannot resist looking back and loses her for ever.

Theseus

Abandoned by his father, Aegeus, king of Athens, as a baby, Theseus, as a young man, returns to Athens to claim his birthright. On the way he encounters many dangers, including the robber, Sinis, who captures travellers and kills them by tying them to two bent-over pine trees, then letting the trees go. Theseus kills Sinis in the same gruesome way.

When Orpheus dies, his head and lyre, still singing, float down the River Hebrus to the Mediterranean Sea (above). His soul finally joins Eurydice in Hades, and his lyre becomes a constellation of stars.

In one of his exploits, Theseus kills the centaur, Eurytus.

12

Many more encounters follow in which Theseus shows great courage, turning the tables on his attackers. When he at last reaches Athens, he keeps his identity secret from his father. But King Aegeus's wife, Medea (see page 8), recognises Theseus and is worried that Aegeus will choose him as his heir, instead of her own son. She tries to have Theseus killed by sending him to capture the ferocious Cretan Bull. But her plan is foiled when Theseus catches the bull and returns, in triumph, to Athens. Medea tries to poison Theseus but, just in time, Aegeus recognises his son's sandals, shield and sword, and knocks the poisoned drink from his hands. Aegeus and Theseus are reconciled and Medea is sent into exile. Later, Theseus heroically kills the dreaded Minotaur (see page 28).

Tales of heroes

Legendary sagas, mostly Viking, but some Pagan and some Christian, tell epic tales of heroes and their deeds from days long ago. They also contain many mythological themes and characters, such as magic, giants, dwarves and elves. Some of the sagas, such as 'Ragnar's Saga', are based both in history and legend. Ragnar Lodbrok was a great Viking chief of the 9th century whose nickname of 'Hairy Breeches' refers to the trousers made for him by his wife. They were said to be made from thick fur, boiled in pitch and rolled in sand, to make them resistant to a dragon's fiery breath. A larger-than-life character, he claimed to be descended from the great god, Odin. The saga tells of his exploits in Scandinavia, and of his raids against France and England. He is finally taken prisoner by the King of Northumbria and thrown into a pit of snakes where he dies.

Many of the sagas tell stories of heroic warriors (above). The Saga of Asmund, the Champion-Killer from Iceland, recounts the fight to the death of two great warriors, Hildebrand and his half-brother, Asmund.

This painting shows a theme common in many legendary sagas – the death of a great hero in battle, after slaying many of his enemies.

Rostam

The Shahnameh is a very long, epic poem, written by the Persian poet, Ferdowsi, in around 1000 AD. It tells the story of Persia's mythological and historical past, and of its heroes. The greatest among these is called Rostam. The son of Zal, a legendary Persian warrior, and Rudaba, a beautiful princess, Rostam is famous for his extraordinary courage and strength. As a child he kills a white elephant with a single blow of his mace and tames a mighty stallion, Rakhsh. After this, no one but Rostam is able to ride the stallion. Later, Rostam has to perform a series of tasks, similar to those of Herakles (see page 10), in order to save his king, who has been captured by demons. These are known as 'Rostam's Seven Labours', and include Rostam fighting beasts, such as lions, demons and dragons (see page 25), with the help of the faithful Rakhsh. The most famous story in the Shahnameh concerns Rostam and Sohrab. Unaware that Sohrab is his son, Rostam fatally wounds him in battle. Only then does he learn the truth.

In this picture, Rostam kills the hero, Esfandyar. Rostam shoots a double-headed arrow into his eyes, his only weak point (see page 44).

Gilgamesh

The mythical hero-king, Gilgamesh, is the main character in the Epic of Gilgamesh, an epic poem from Ancient Mesopotamia. The son of a king, it is said that Gilgamesh's mother was a goddess. The story centres around the friendship between Gilgamesh and the wild man, Enkidu. Originally, Enkidu is sent to kill Gilgamesh but the two respect each other's strength and become friends.

Together, they undertake a series of dangerous quests, including fighting monsters and giant bulls. When Enkidu dies, Gilgamesh is distraught. He realises that he, too, will die one day and begins to search for the secret of immortality. From Utnapishtim, the survivor of the Great Flood, Gilgamesh hears about a plant that grows at the bottom of a lake in the Underworld and grants eternal life. He finds the plant but, on his way back home, it is stolen and eaten by a snake. Gilgamesh returns home a broken man, having lost both his friend and his only chance of immortality.

Early in his rule, Gilgamesh treats his subjects very badly and they pray to the gods for help. The gods make Enkidu out of clay and send him to kill Gilgamesh. The two fight and Gilgamesh defeats Enkidu but spares his life, and the two become friends.

Sinbad the Sailor

The epic story of Sinbad the sailor originates in the ancient Middle East. It tells of the fantastic adventures of the hero, Sinbad, a fictional sailor from Basrah (in modern-day Iraq). Sinbad's travels take the form of seven incredible sea voyages. On the first, Sinbad takes to the sea to earn back the fortune left to him by his father. He lands on an island which proves to be a gigantic whale and becomes separated from his ship. On his second voyage, Sinbad finds himself stranded in a land of giant birds, called 'rocs', said to be large enough to carry off and eat elephants. At the end of each voyage, Sinbad returns home safely, laden with riches. The stories are based partly on folk tales and partly on the real-life experiences of sailors exploring the lands around the Indian Ocean.

On his fifth voyage, Sinbad passes an island on which he spots a gigantic egg, belonging to a roc. To Sinbad's annoyance, the crew break the egg open and eat the chick inside.

Houyi

Chinese mythology tells how, long ago, there were ten suns, the children of Dijun, the God of the Eastern Heaven. For a while, the suns take it in turn to rise but they soon grow tired of this and decide to appear all at once. The resulting heat is terrible – the ground grows parched, crops wilt, and lakes and rivers dry up. Eventually, the Emperor of China asks Dijun for help. Dijun calls for Houyi, the god of archery, and asks him to teach the suns a lesson. But, appalled at how much people have suffered, Houyi shoots down all of the suns but one. The people on Earth are delighted and hail Houyi as a hero but Dijun is furious. As punishment, he banishes Houyi from the heavens and strips him of his immortality.

Houyi saves the Earth by shooting down the suns.

Houyi then sets off on a series of epic adventures, killing many monsters to save China. Although he likes living on Earth, Houyi fears mortality. After a long quest, Houyi finds the elixir of immortality but leaves it at home when he is urgently called on another quest. Unaware of what it is, his wife drinks it and she rises to the moon to live there forever. The loss of his wife changes Houyi and he becomes a tyrant, hated by the people. He is eventually killed by a former student.

Maya Hero Twins

The Popol Vuh, or 'Book of the Community', contains the Mayan story of creation, their history and their myths. Central to the book are the exploits of the mythical Hero Twins – Xbalanque and Hunahpu.

Hun Hunahpu, the father of the Hero Twins, and his brother, Vucub Hunahpu, are summoned to Xibalba, the Underworld, and challenged to a ball game by the lords of death. The lords win the game, kill the brothers and hang Hun Hunahpu's head from a tree. When the daughter of one of the lords approaches the tree, the skull spits in her palm. She becomes pregnant and some time later gives birth to the Hero Twins.

Like their father, the Hero Twins become great ball-players, and vow to avenge his death. Once more, the Lords of Xibalba summon them to play. The Twins cross the river of corruption and the river of blood, and enter the Underworld. Each night, the Lords make them stay in one of the dreadful houses of Xibalba and each night the Twins survive to play the ball game the next day.

Finally, in the House of Bats, the Twins sleep inside their blowpipes so that they do not get bitten. But when Hunahpu pokes out his head to see if dawn has broken, a bat snatches his head and carries it to the ball court. When the game begins, Hunahpu has a new head made from a squash and his real head is used as a ball. To the Lords' fury, the Twins are victorious.

Eventually, the twins allow themselves to be killed and ground into bones and dust. This is, however, all part of their plan. When their bodies are thrown into a river, they come back to life, first as a pair of catfish, then as a pair of young boys again. They return, unrecognised, to the court of the Lords of Xibalba where they perform a miracle by killing a person and then bringing him back to life. When the victim tells of how wonderful the experience was, the Lords demand that they should have this miracle performed on them. The Twins kill the Lords of Xibalba but do not bring them back to life. After getting their revenge the twins rise into the sky to become the Sun and the Moon.

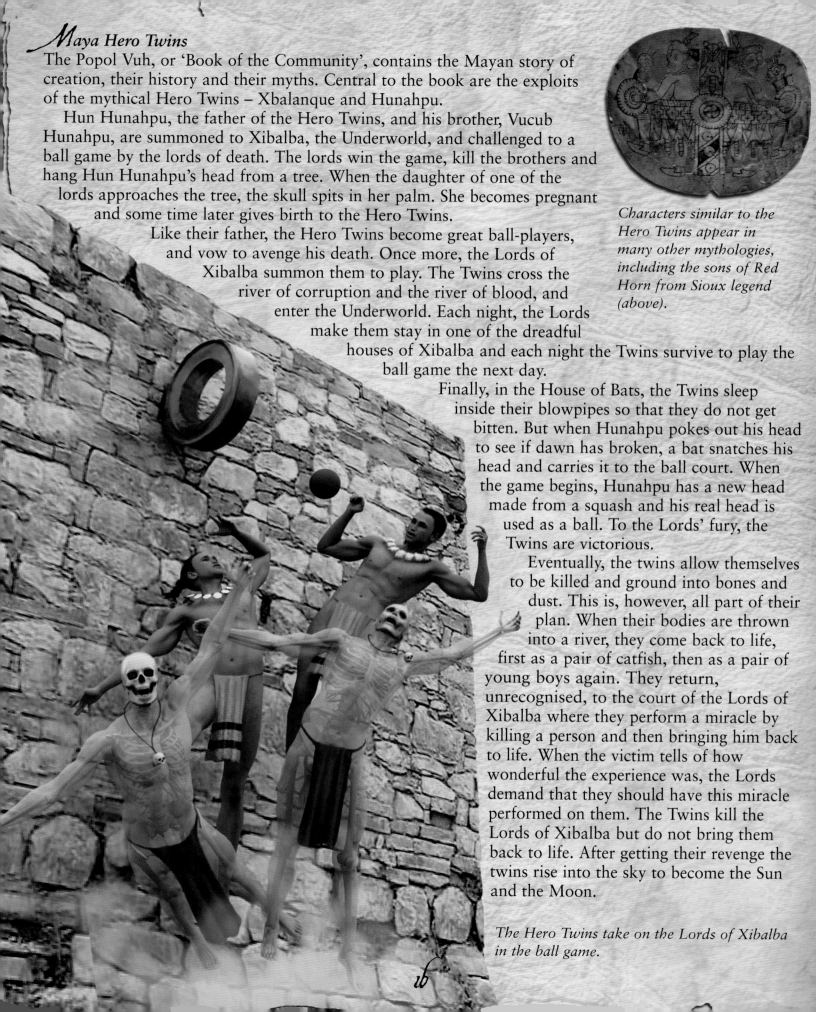

Characters similar to the Hero Twins appear in many other mythologies, including the sons of Red Horn from Sioux legend (above).

The Hero Twins take on the Lords of Xibalba in the ball game.

Knights of the Round Table

In British mythology, many epic tales are told of the Knights of the Round Table. This group of men were the most noble and highly regarded knights at the court of King Arthur (see pages 18-19). They were believed to meet at a table that had no head nor foot to show that all the knights who sat around it were of equal importance.

One of the most famous of the knights was Sir Lancelot. Stories of his life and adventures appear in many medieval works. Legend says that Lancelot was raised by the mythical Lady of the Lake, after the death of his father. She sends him to Arthur's court where he becomes a knight and embarks on a series of heroic adventures and quests, including rescuing Queen Guinevere from Arthur's enemy, Meleagant. A brave and skilful swordsman, Lancelot becomes the king's champion, fighting challenges in Arthur's name. But his reputation is tarnished when he falls in love with Guinevere. Together with his son, Sir Galahad, and Sir Perceval, Lancelot takes part in the quest for the Holy Grail, a plate or cup said to have been used by Jesus Christ at the Last Supper. It is ultimately the gallant and pure Sir Galahad who finds the Grail.

Apart from his heroic exploits, Lancelot is famous for his love affair with Guinevere, Arthur's wife (below). When Arthur discovers them he sentences Guinevere to death, but she is rescued by Lancelot.

The picture below shows three knights of the Round Table – Galahad, Bors and Perceval – finally finding the Holy Grail after a long and difficult quest.

A young Arthur pulls the sword from the stone, proving that he is the rightful king. 18

Hero Kings

The hero king is a well-known figure of legend, keeping his kingdom safe and ridding it of war, pestilence and monsters. The most famous example is undoubtedly King Arthur, whose existence owes more to folklore than it does to historical fact.

On Bran the Blessed's command, his men cut off his head but it continues to speak to them for seven years until they reach London and bury it. There, it protects Britain from invaders.

King Arthur

The first reliable account of Arthur comes from a Welsh work written in the 9th century AD. But it was the writings of Geoffrey of Monmouth, 300 years later, that really laid down the foundations of the legend. Arthur appears as the son of King Uther Pendragon and heir to the throne. When Uther dies, there is conflict over who should succeed him. Merlin, a wise magician, sets a sword in a block of stone. Whoever can draw the sword out of the stone will become King of England. Arthur manages this easily and establishes his court at the legendary Camelot.

The Fianna welcome their leader, Fionn mac Cumhaill (Finn McCool).

Celtic Kings

Celtic mythology features many stories of heroic kings. In Welsh legend, the giant, Bran the Blessed, is King of Britain. His great strength and stature make him a formidable opponent in battle. He and seven of his men survive a bloody war against the Irish but Bran is mortally wounded in the fighting.

The Irish hero, Fionn mac Cumhaill (Finn McCool), is leader of a band of warriors called the Fianna. A giant, as well as heroic figure, there are many legends about his life. Among them is the story of how he becomes leader after killing the fire-breathing fairy, Aillen, with his magical spear.

Agamemnon

In Greek mythology, Agamemnon is the son of King Atreus of Mycenae, and brother of Menelaus. When Helen, wife of Menelaus, is kidnapped by Paris of Troy, Agamemnon becomes commander of the Greek army and leads them heroically in the Trojan War (see pages 34-35). On his return, Agamemnon is invited to a banquet by his wife, Clytemnestra, and her lover, Aegisthus, and is murdered. His death is later avenged by his son, Orestes, and daughter, Electra, who kill their mother.

On his return from Troy, Agamemnon is murdered by Clytemnestra and Aegisthus (left).

Romulus

The famous story of Romulus and his brother, Remus, appears in Roman mythology. The twin sons of Mars, god of war, they are abandoned as babies in the River Tiber but are rescued by a she-wolf. Later, they are found and raised by a shepherd, Faustulus, and his wife. After revealing their true identity as the sons of Mars, the brothers found a new city on the banks of the Tiber but soon afterwards, Romulus kills Remus in a quarrel. The city is named Rome, after Romulus, who becomes its first king.

As king, Romulus sets about enlarging the city and expanding its power and influence. At first, the only citizens of Rome are men, followers of Romulus. To solve this problem, Romulus invites the neighbouring Sabine people to a festival, then kidnaps all of the women. This leads to years of fighting between the Romans and the Sabines.

After his death, Romulus is made into a god, Quirinus, who represents the people and city of Rome. As Quirinus, he is shown as a warrior, dressed for battle and holding a spear.

Fearing that they will threaten his power, Romulus and Remus's uncle, King Amulius, orders his servant to kill the twin babies. Instead, the servant puts them in a basket on the River Tiber. Legend says that the gods kept them safe until they were discovered and raised by a she-wolf.

Prince Cadmus

A hero of Phoenician and Greek mythology, Prince Cadmus is sent by his parents to find and rescue his sister, Europa, after she is abducted by the god, Zeus. He is told not to return without her. Unsuccessful in his quest, Cadmus's wanderings take him to Delphi in Greece, where he consults the Oracle. The Oracle tells him to give up his search and, instead, to follow a cow with a half-moon mark on her side, and to build a city on the spot where she lies down. Cadmus follows the Oracle's instructions and founds the city of Thebes. On the way some of his companions are killed by a dragon which in turn is killed by Cadmus. He plants the dragon's teeth in the ground and they sprout into fierce warriors who help him to build the city, and become the ancestors of the noblest Theban families.

Cadmus is instructed to plant the dragon's teeth by the goddess, Athena. When the warriors grow, Cadmus throws a stone into them so that they start fighting amongst themselves (a trick that is used by the Greek hero Jason in his quest for the Golden Fleece). The five survivors help him to build Thebes.

A statue of Hayk in Yerevan, the capital of Armenia.

Hayk, the Hero

The legendary hero king, Hayk, is revered as the founder of the country of Armenia. According to ancient accounts, he was a man of gigantic stature, a fearless warrior and a mighty archer. At one time, Hayk and his people settle in Babylon but the region is ruled by a terrible giant, called Bel. Bel tries to subdue Hayk's people but proud Hayk refuses to give in to him and become his slave. A great battle follows in which Bel sends a huge force against Hayk. Hayk kills Bel with his long bow and Bel's army is sent fleeing.

Herakles battles with the Lernaean Hydra.

Monster Slayers

Battling against fearsome beasts is the true stuff of hero myths. Many-headed dragons, giants, demons, gorgons and minotaurs are just some of the terrifying monsters to fall prey to mythical heroes.

Legend says that St George killed a dragon which was about to devour one of the king's daughters. The myth was probably brought back to Europe from the Middle East by Christian knights during the Crusades.

Susanoo slaying the eight-headed dragon, Yamata no Orochi.

Dragon Slayers

For his second labour, Herakles, the most famous Greek hero, is sent to kill the Lernaean Hydra. This hideous monster has nine heads and deadly poisonous breath. Each time Herakles cuts one head off, another two grow in its place. Herakles calls on his nephew, Iolaus, for help. After each head is cut off, Iolaus seals the stump with a burning branch until, at last, the Hydra is dead.

Slaying many-headed dragons was not solely the task of Greek heroes. In Japanese mythology, the storm god, Susanoo, must battle the eight-headed dragon, Yamata no Orochi. Banished to Earth, Susanoo meets an elderly couple whose seven daughters have already been eaten by the dragon. They ask for his help in saving their eighth child. Susanoo leaves eight buckets of strong liquor for the dragon to drink and it falls into a drunken stupor. As it sleeps, Susanoo kills it and cuts it into pieces, discovering a magic sword (see page 41) in its tail.

Saving princesses from dragons has become one of a hero's most famous tasks. The medieval story of St George is similar to many earlier myths from Ancient Greece. On his way home from killing Medusa (see page 28), Perseus sees the beautiful Andromeda, daughter of King Cepheus and Queen Cassiopeia, who is about to be sacrificed to a terrifying sea dragon. Heroically, Perseus slays the dragon and marries Andromeda.

Perseus arrives just in time to save Andromeda from the sea dragon.

Cadmus and the sacred dragon

After slaying the water dragon (see page 21), Prince Cadmus is followed by ill fortune. The dragon is sacred to the god, Ares, who makes Cadmus serve him for eight years as penance. One day, Cadmus remarks that the gods seem particularly fond of dragons and that he wishes that he could be one. At once, his body starts to change into that of a dragon and he begins to grow scales.

Sigurd and Fafnir

In Norse mythology, Fafnir was the son of a dwarf king. Immensely strong and ruthless, he is given the task of guarding his father's hoard of gold. Later, as his greed for gold grows, he turns himself into a dragon so that he can guard it better. Regin, Fafnir's brother, sends Sigurd to kill the dragon using a powerful sword he has forged. The young hero succeeds in slaying the dragon by plunging the sword into its heart. He eats the dragon's heart which gives him the ability to understand the animals. In this way, he learns from the birds that Regin is planning to murder him and steal the gold, so Sigurd kills him first.

Cadmus and the dragon painted on a Greek vase

Sigurd kills the dragon, Fafnir (left).

Beowulf lies mortally wounded next to the slain dragon (below).

Beowulf's last fight

The great hero, Beowulf, appears in an Anglo-Saxon epic of the same name, written in Old English. He is a warrior of a people called the Geats, who lived in southern Sweden. Late in Beowulf's life, a dragon attacks the Geats in revenge for the theft of some of its treasure. Beowulf and his faithful companion, Wiglaf, succeed in slaying the dragon but Beowulf is mortally wounded and dies.

Haymo, the giant

In the legend of Haymo, a ferocious dragon guards a hoard of gold on a mountain near Innsbruck, Austria. During a storm, some of the dragon's gold is washed down the mountain, where local people gather it up. Furious, the dragon destroys everything in its path. Haymo, a giant, tracks down the dragon and kills it, cutting off its tongue as proof.

Haymo cuts off the dragon's tongue as proof of his heroic deed.

Dobrynya and Gorynych

Dobrynya is a famous dragon-slaying hero of Russian mythology. A dragon from the Saracen Mountains, called Gorynych, captures Zabava, the niece of a local prince. The prince calls on Dobrynya, who fights the dragon using a magic whip. After three days, Dobrynya kills the dragon but the dragon's blood does not soak into the ground. Dobrynya and his horse are stuck fast until a voice tells him to stick his spear in the ground and recite a spell. This sets Dobrynya free and he is, at last, able to rescue Zabava and return her home.

Rostam is saved from a dragon by Rakhsh

On his travels, the hero Rostam (see page 14) stops for a rest, only to be discovered by a dragon. Rostam's trusty horse, Rakhsh, wakes him up but Rostam cannot see the danger. This happens again, and again, and Rostam is furious at being disturbed. The third time, Rostam sees the dragon and slays it, with Rakhsh's help.

Dobrynya rescues Zabava from the dragon, Gorynych (above).

Rostam and Rakhsh fight a dragon (below).

Giant killers of the ancient world

There are many stories of heroes encountering giants in the mythologies of Ancient Greece and Rome. On his journey to Athens, Theseus kills the giant, Sinis (see pages 12–13). He ties the giant between two bent trees, then lets the trees go, tearing Sinis apart – the same way Sinis had killed his own victims.

Theseus kills Sinis.

Antaeus is a giant from Greek mythology, said to be the son of the god, Poseidon, and the goddess, Gaia. He is immensely strong but only if he remains in contact with the ground. The hero, Herakles, challenges Antaeus to a wrestling match and lifts him into the air, thus robbing him of his strength so that he can kill him. Herakles also kills the fire-breathing giant, Cacus. On his return journey from killing the giant Geryon and taking his cattle, Herakles takes a nap near the cave where Cacus lives. Cacus steals some of the cattle and hides them in his cave. When Herakles discovers this he breaks into the cave and slays the giant.

On his journey back to Iolcus after seizing the Golden Fleece (see page 8), Jason must overcome many obstacles, including the great bronze giant, Talos, who protects the island of Crete by hurling rocks at approaching ships. Talos has one vein, running from his neck to his ankle, pinned shut by a single bronze nail. Medea hypnotises Talos so that he stumbles and dislodges the nail. Then his blood, made of lead, flows out and he dies.

Talos dislodges the nail in his ankle, leading to his death.

Herakles and Cacus

Corineus
throws the giant, Goemagot,
over a cliff and into the sea.

In King Arthur's battle with
the giant, he must dodge the
giant's huge club. Eventually,
blood from a cut to the giant's
forehead blinds him, and
Arthur is able to take
advantage and kill him.

Corineus and Goemagot

In legend, Corineus is a great warrior, who accompanies Brutus, a Trojan, to England, where he becomes King of Cornwall. At that time, Cornwall, in southern England, was inhabited by giants. It is said that Corineus wrestles with Goemagot (or Gogmagog), the greatest of the giants, then kills him by hurling him over a cliff, now known as Gogmagog's Leap.

Gilgamesh and Humbaba

In the Epic of Gilgamesh (see page 14) from Ancient Sumeria, Humbaba is a gigantic monster that guards the Cedar Forest, where the gods live. It is said to have a face of coiled intestines and breath of fire, but it is no match for Gilgamesh and Enkidu. While on a raid with 50 men to cut down trees from the Cedar Forest, Gilgamesh distracts Humbaba and Enkidu cuts off the monster's head.

Knights and giants

Tales of knights doing battle with giants are a common feature in the folklore of Wales, Scotland and Ireland. Giants also appear in legends associated with King Arthur (see page 19). In one story, Arthur kills a giant in an epic fight on Mont Saint-Michel (left).

The legendary knight, Roland, is a character from European myth (see pages 32-33). One version of his story tells of Roland's heroic battle with a giant, called Ferragus, who seems to be invulnerable. After a long sword fight, the two pause to get their breath and sit down to talk. During their long conversation, Ferragus tells Roland that he has only one weak spot – in his navel. When the fight resumes, Roland stabs Ferragus in the place he has pointed out, and kills the giant.

Gilgamesh faces the
monstrous Humbaba,
guardian of the Cedar Forest.

Roland and the giant,
Ferragus, fight each other.

Bellerophon slays the Chimera

One of the greatest monster-slayers of Ancient Greece is the hero, Bellerophon. As a young man, Bellerophon is banished and sent to King Iobates of Lycia. Instead of killing Bellerophon, the king sends him on a quest. He must slay the fearsome Chimera, a monster that is part-lion, part-goat and part-snake. To help Bellerophon in his task, the goddess, Athena, gives him the winged horse, Pegasus, to ride. Bellerophon is able to fly down on the Chimera and kill the hideous creature with his spear.

Bellerophon and Pegasus battle the Chimera.

Perseus kills Medusa

Medusa was one of three hideous monsters, called Gorgons, whose hair was a mass of writhing snakes. Their glance was so powerful that anyone who looked at them was immediately turned into stone. Perseus (see page 25), vows to kill Medusa in order to prove his courage and asks the gods for help. Among other magical items, they give him a pair of winged sandals, a sickle, a helmet of invisibility, and a shining bronze shield. When Perseus finds Medusa, he hovers above her on his winged sandals. Then, looking at her reflection in the shield, he uses the sickle to cut her head off.

After killing Medusa, Perseus flees, chased by Medusa's sisters. He escapes by wearing the helmet of invisibility, given to him by the gods.

Theseus and the Minotaur

The hero, Theseus, features in one of the most famous Greek myths (see pages 12-13). Every nine years, King Minos of Crete demands that Athens send 14 young people to be fed to the Minotaur, a terrible beast with the head of a bull and a man's body that lives in a maze-like labyrinth in his palace. Theseus volunteers to be one of the victims. Entering the labyrinth, he pulls out the sword that he had hidden, and kills the dreaded Minotaur. Then he uses a thread of string, given to him by Ariadne, to find his way out of the labyrinth again, leading the other Athenians to safety.

A picture showing Meleager killing the Calydonian boar (right), after it has been wounded with an arrow by Atalanta, one of the few heroines in mythology. The other hunters are angry that the prize of the boar's hide is awarded to a woman.

Theseus tracks down the minotaur in its Labyrinth then kills it, freeing the captive Athenians soon after.

Hunting the giant boar

Greek myths tell of a monstrous boar sent by the gods to terrorise the region of Calydon. King Oeneus sends his son, Meleager, to gather together all the heroes of Greece in order to hunt the boar. But the hunters also include a woman, called Atalanta, and it is she who first wounds the boar, enabling Meleager to kill it. As a reward, she is given the boar's hide. This angers the other hunters, who try to take the hide from her. The struggle ends tragically with the death of several of the heroes, including Meleager.

Oedipus and the Sphinx

On his travels to Thebes, Oedipus, a prince, meets the Sphinx, a monster that sets travellers a riddle. If they answer correctly, they are allowed to continue on their way. If they give the wrong answer, the Sphinx kills them. The riddle is: 'What walks on four feet in the morning, two at noon, and three at night?' Oedipus is the first person to give the correct answer: 'A human being, who crawls on all fours as a baby, walks upright on two legs as an adult, and leans on a walking stick in old age.' Astonished, the Sphinx throws herself to her death from a clifftop.

Oedipus encounters the Sphinx, a winged monster with the body of a lion and the head of a woman.

Ahaiyuta and the Cloud Eater

Zuni Indian folklore tells of the Cloud Eater, a monster as tall as a mountain that devours every cloud in the sky, causing a terrible drought. Many brave men have tried to track the Cloud Eater down and kill him, but none has succeeded. A boy, called Ahaiyuta, decides to try his luck, helped by four magic feathers – red, blue, yellow and black – given to him by his grandmother. The red feather guides him in the right direction and soon he meets a ground squirrel. The blue feather gives him the power to talk to the squirrel; the yellow feather allows him to shrink down to fit inside the ground squirrel's burrow. Finally, with the ground squirrel's help, Ahaiyuta reaches the Cloud Eater's home. Putting the black feather in his hair, he is able to kill the monster, and bring clouds and rain back to the world.

The Maya Hero Twins and Vucub Caquix

Mayan mythology tells many stories of the exploits of the Hero Twins, Hunahpu and Xbalanque (see page 16). After a terrible flood leaves the world in twilight, a monstrous bird called Vucub Caquix claims, falsely, to be the god of the Sun and the Moon. To teach him a lesson, Hunahpu shoots him out of his tree with his blowpipe. In the struggle, Vucub Caquix wrenches Hunahpu's arm off and escapes. But the Twins later trick him into giving away his teeth, his eyes, and his riches and so he loses his power.

Ahaiyuta and the ground squirrel encounter the dreadful Cloud Eater in Zuni Indian legend (right).

Hunahpu prepares to shoot the monster bird, Vucub Caquix (left).

The hero, Beowulf, tears the arm from the monster, Grendel.

Beowulf and Grendel

For many years, King Hrothgar's palace of Heorot and his people have been under attack from a monster, called Grendel. The monster is angered by the singing and celebrations that he can hear coming from the great hall. In revenge, he attacks the hall, then kills and eats many of Hrothgar's warriors as they are sleeping.

The great warrior, Beowulf (see page 24), hears of King Hrothgar's plight and offers to fight Grendel. He and his men spend the night in the palace, although Beowulf only pretends to sleep. When Grendel attacks, Beowulf fights him and tears off his arm. Then Grendel crawls back home to the marsh to die.

But the battle is not over yet. During the night, Grendel's fearsome mother arrives at the palace to avenge the death of her son. Beowulf follows her to the marsh to fight her but cannot kill her with his own sword. Instead, he takes a magic sword from her own hoard and slays her. Peace is restored to Heorot, and Beowulf is rewarded for his heroism with horses and gold.

The demon, Hidimba, and the hero, Bhima, fight to the death in the forest.

Bhima fights a Rakshasa

In the Hindu epic poem, the Mahabharata, Bhima is one of the Pandava brothers, famous for his extraordinary size and strength. It is said that Bhima is so strong that he can fight 60,000 warriors at once. For a time, Bhima and his brothers live in exile in the forest. A rakshasa (demon) brother and sister, called Hidimba and Hidimbi, also live in the forest and try to lure the brothers into a trap so that they can eat them. Bhima sees through their plan and uses his great strength to kill Hidimba, saving his brothers' lives.

Warrior Heroes

In myths and legends from around the world, heroes often find themselves pitted against each other in great battles and conflicts. Often, in the face of danger or adversity, or from a position of weakness, heroes must display not only courage but also self-sacrifice.

Last-ditch stands

Many heroes face their deaths in desperate, last-ditch stands. At Roncevaux Pass, Roland (see page 27), fights a losing battle against a force greatly outnumbering his small rearguard. Roland's faithful friend, Oliver, advises him to blow his legendary olifant (ivory) hunting horn to call Charlemagne's main force back to help. Roland refuses and all his men are killed. Fatally wounded, he finally blows the horn, so that his death can be avenged.

Horatius Cocles jumps into the river after holding back the enemy.

In Celtic mythology, the great hero, Cu Chulainn, is killed after his spirit is weakened by trickery. He is mortally wounded by a magic spear thrown by his enemy, Lugaid. Realising that he is near death, Cu Chulainn straps himself to a standing stone so that he can die on his feet. Such is his reputation, it is only when a crow lands on his shoulder that his enemies finally believe he is dead.

Not all heroes perish in last-ditch stands. During an attack by the Etruscans on the city of Rome, an army officer, Horatio Cocles, saves the day and survives. Cocles and his men are guarding the Sublicius Bridge as the Etruscans try to swarm across. As his men desert their posts, Cocles advances to the head of the bridge with two men to keep the enemy at bay. Meanwhile, he orders others to start destroying the bridge. As the bridge collapses, Cocles sends back his companions and holds off the enemy on his own. Finally, despite being badly wounded, he jumps into the river and manages to swim to the shore.

Cu Chulainn dies standing on his feet like a hero, tied to a standing stone.

Heroes of the Trojan War

In Greek mythology, the Trojan War was waged by the Greeks against the city of Troy when Paris, Prince of Troy, stole the beautiful Helen from her husband, King Menelaus of Sparta. Furious, Menelaus vows revenge, preparing and arming a fleet of one thousand ships to go to war against Troy. The fleet is commanded by Menelaus's brother, the great warrior, Agamemnon (see page 20). For ten years the Greeks lay seige to Troy, with the deaths of many heroes on both sides, including the Greeks, Achilles and Ajax, and the Trojans, Hector and Paris.

One of the most famous Greek heroes is Achilles. Achilles is invulnerable, apart from one place on his body – his heel (see page 44). Grief-stricken by the death of Patroclus at the hands of Hector, Paris's brother, Achilles kills Hector and drags his body around the city behind his chariot. It is Paris who avenges Hector's death by shooting an arrow into Achilles' heel.

Diomedes is another outstanding warrior within the Greek army. Famed for his strength, he even beats the mighty Ajax in a sparring contest. In battle, he wounds the great Trojan hero, Aeneas, then dares to wound the goddess, Aphrodite, as she tries to save her son.

Ajax, the Greek hero, is described as being immensely tall and strong. When Achilles is killed, Ajax fights off the Trojans until Odysseus can drag Achilles's body away.

Diomedes wounds Aphrodite as she protects Aeneas.

With many of their heroes dead, the Greeks are told that only the famous archer, Philoctetes, can save them. At first, Philoctetes refuses because the Greeks had already left him behind when he was bitten by a snake. Assured by Herakles that his wound would heal, Philoctetes finally goes to Troy, where he kills Paris with a single shot.

Troy finally falls because of a cunning trick devised by Odysseus (see page 7). He tells the Greeks to pretend to surrender and sail away. Then he fills a huge wooden horse with soldiers and leaves it by the gates of Troy, as a gift for the goddess, Athena. As planned, the Trojans drag the horse inside the city. As they celebrate their victory, however, the Greek soldiers climb out, open the city gates and let in the Greek army.

Aeneas escapes from Troy with his father and son, and flees to Italy.

The Greeks ransack Troy and kill great numbers of Trojans. One of the few who are allowed to escape is the Trojan hero, Aeneas (see page 9).

The gods are very angry over the destruction of their temples by the Acheans and decide that most would not return home. A storm falls on the returning fleet and many are shipwrecked. It takes some survivors, such as Odysseus, ten years to return home (see page 7).

Penthesilea, Queen of the Amazons, fights with her warriors on the side of the Trojans. She is killed by Achilles, who later realises that he is in love with her.

This carving (left) shows the five Pandava princes, heroes of the Mahabharata, and their wife, Draupadi. From left to right: Bhima, Arjuna, Yudhisthira and the twins, Nakula and Sahadeva. Draupadi stands to the far right.

Heroes of the Kurukshetra War

The great Indian epic poem, the Mahabharata, centres around the rivalry between two ruling families – the Pandavas and the Kauravas. When King Pandu dies, he leaves his throne to his eldest son, Yudhisthira. But he and his four brothers (the Pandavas) have rivals for power in their cousins (the Kauravas). At first, the Kauravas cheat the Pandavas out of their kingdom in a game of dice and banish them. The Pandavas later return and demand their rightful place. Finally, the two sides meet at Kurukshetra in northern India to fight a bloody battle that lasts for 18 days.

Before the battle begins, Krishna, an incarnation of the god Vishnu, meets with the leaders of each side – Yudhisthira's brother, Arjuna, for the Pandavas, and Duryodhana for the Kauravas. Krishna is himself a great warrior and has a large army of his own. He offers Arjuna and Duryodhana a choice – they can either have his army or his help in person. Duryodhana chooses the army. Arjuna chooses Krishna, who becomes Arjuna's charioteer.

A skilful archer and a brave but gentle man, Arjuna does not really want to go to war, especially against his relations. Krishna reminds him that it is his duty and cannot be avoided.

In this statue (left), Arjuna is shown displaying his great skill, archery.

The Kauravas attack the mighty Bhima with all of their force. Bhima fights back, killing several of Duryodhana's brothers until he is wounded by an arrow.

As battle commences, the two sides face each other. Bhishma, grandfather to both the Pandavas and Kauravas, is fighting on the Kauravas' side. He fights bravely, causing havoc and great losses in the Pandavan ranks. Arjuna realises that he must act quickly to kill Bhishma and a fierce battle rages. But it is ultimately Arjuna's friend, Satyaki, who kills Bhishma's charioteer so that his horses bolt, taking Bhishma away from the battlefield.

On the fourth day of battle the mighty Bhima (see page 31), Arjuna's brother, demonstrates his heroic bravery. With Arjuna's son, Abhimanyu, surrounded by Kauravas, Bhima appears and starts swinging his mace at the enemy soldiers. In response, Duryodhana sends a herd of elephants to trample Bhima. But Bhima scatters them single-handedly. Duryodhana orders an all-out attack but Bhima again proves his strength, killing many of the Kauravas until he is finally hit by an arrow. It is now his son, the much-feared Ghatotkacha, who takes up the fight, sending the Kauravas fleeing.

For days, the battle rages with terrible loss of life on each side. On day ten, Arjuna realises that he must find another way of stopping Bhishma. He sends Shikhandi, who was a woman in a previous life, to kill Bhishma, as Bhishma has vowed never to attack a woman. Shikhandi fires arrow after arrow at Bhishma, until he falls from his chariot and dies.

This painting (right) shows a dying Bhishma with Krishna and the Pandavas. His body is held off the ground by the arrows sticking out of it.

By the 18th day of the war, tens of thousands of soldiers lie dead but the Pandavas are finally close to victory. Realising that defeat is near, Duryodhana flees from the battlefield and takes refuge in a lake. But Bhima soon catches up with him and challenges him to a fight in which Duryodhana is mortally wounded. As he dies, his loyal followers vow to avenge his death. Later that night, they attack the Pandava's camp and kill the remaining soldiers they find there.

At the end of the war, only 12 warriors survive, including the five Pandava brothers and Krishna. Yudhisthira is crowned king and rules for many years, before passing the throne to Arjuna's grandson, Parikshit. Then, with Krishna's blessing, Yudhisthira and his brothers set off on a pilgrimage to the Himalayas, to make amends for all the killing.

Knight-errant

A painting showing a group of Russian knight-errants, with heroic Ilya Muromets in the centre.

In medieval tales, the knight-errant was a knight who wandered in search of adventure in order to prove his bravery and worth. Typical quests include daring deeds, such as rescuing maidens in distress and slaying dragons. In Russian mythology, Ilya Muromets, along with Dobrynya Nikitich and Alyosha Popovich (see page 25), is the most famous knight-errant of all. The son of a farmer, Ilya is given superhuman powers by a dying knight, and sets out to save the city of Kiev from invasion. On the way, he single-handedly defends the city of Chernigov from nomadic invasion and slays a terrifying monster that kills travellers with a whistle.

Starkad

Starkad was a hero of Norse mythology. A great warrior, he was famed for his enormous size and strength. He was said to be capable of great deeds but also of doing great evil. A Danish version of the story tells how, when Starkad is very old, he hangs his gold around his neck and sets out to die. Eventually, he tells a warrior called Hather to kill him by cutting off his head.

Starkad appears in many sagas and legends, killing kings and warriors.

Hua Mulan

Hua Mulan

The story of Hua Mulan appears in a 6th-century Chinese poem, the Song of Mulan. In war-torn China, hundreds of thousands of men are called up to join the army. Disguised as a man, Hua Mulan, the heroine, takes her father's place and fights bravely for ten years, winning promotion to general. One day, in a surprise attack, Mulan is wounded by an arrow. She goes to recover at the home of Han Mei, a girl whom she has saved. When Mulan is better, she prepares to go back to the battlefield. But Han Mei tells Mulan that she wants to marry her and Mulan is forced to reveal her true identity.

Like Song Jiang, Yang Lin (right) is another outlaw from the Water Margin. Nicknamed 'Multi-coloured leopard', he is often armed with a large iron spear.

Robin Hood (left) is a popular outlaw of folklore, hiding out in Sherwood Forest during medieval times.

Outlaw heroes

There are many stories of heroic outlaws, forced to live separately from society because of some crime or misdeed. The Chinese novel, the Water Margin, tells of the exploits of a group of 108 outlaws in the 12th century. It is based on the adventures of a real-life outlaw, Song Jiang, and his companions. Song Jiang becomes a fugitive after killing his wife.

The best known outlaw in the West is probably Robin Hood. A hero of English folk tales, he is a highly-skilled archer, famous for stealing from the rich and giving to the poor. Legend tells how he lives in the forest, with his band of 'Merry Men'. It is not known if Robin was a historical figure, although some stories link him to the Earl of Huntingdon.

Folk hero, William Tell, famed for his skill with a crossbow, is said to have lived in Switzerland in the early 14th century. Tell is arrested by the overlord for not showing him respect. He is forced to shoot an apple off the head of his son, Walter, or both of them will be executed. Tell splits the apple open with one shot from his crossbow but he is not freed as promised. Later, he escapes and shoots the overlord, sparking off a rebellion and forcing him to live as an outlaw.

William Tell

Magical Weapons and Armour

In many cases, heroes are able to gain an advantage over their enemies with the help of some magic, usually in the form of magical weapons or armour. Sometimes, this can make them invulnerable to ordinary weapons. However, they often have a weak spot that can lead to their ultimate downfall.

The Norse hero, Sigurd, kills the dragon, Fafnir, with a sword, called Gram. It was forged by Regin from the fragments of a sword belonging to Sigurd's father, Sigmund.

Yamato Takeru uses the magic powers of Kusanagi-no-Tsurugi.

Magical swords

One of the most famous magical swords in Western mythology is Excalibur. Legend says that King Arthur received the sword from the Lady of the Lake and that it was returned to the lake by Sir Bedivere when Arthur died. The blade was said to be bright enough to blind Arthur's enemies, and the scabbard prevented the wearer's wounds from bleeding.

In Japanese mythology, a sword, called Kusanagi-no-Tsurugi (grass-cutting sword), rivalled Excalibur's importance. The wind god, Susanoo (see page 23), discovers the sword inside the tail of an eight-headed monster he slays. He gives it to the goddess, Amaterasu, to settle an old grievance. Later, the sword is given to the great warrior-hero, Yamato Takeru, by his aunt, to protect him from danger. This it does, brilliantly. An enemy warlord lures Yamato into grassland, then starts to set fire to the grass with his burning arrows. Using the sword, Yamato cuts back the grass and directs the winds to blow the fire back towards the warlord and his men.

Norse legends tell the story of another magic sword, called Tyrfing. Its first owner is King Svafrlamli who forces two dwarves to forge a sword with a golden hilt, that will never rust, will cut through stone and iron, and will never miss a stroke. The dwarves, Dvalinn and Durin, do as they are asked but, in revenge, they curse the sword so that it will cause great evil and will, eventually, kill Svafrlamli himself.

Svafrlamli takes possession of the sword, Tyrfing.

Gae Bulg

The Gae Bulg, or 'notched spear', is the magical spear belonging to the Irish hero, Cu Chulainn (see page 33). Made from the bones of a sea monster, it is given to him by his teacher, a warrior woman, called Scathach. Cu Chulainn is the only person who knows the technique of using it. Legend says that, when the spear enters a person's body, it opens into a series of sharp barbs which are impossible to remove. The spear is only used as a last resort, as it always proves fatal once it is thrown. On one occasion, Cu Chulainn uses the Gae Bulg in a fight against Ferdiad, his foster brother. The fight lasts for three days, until Cu Chulainn calls on his charioteer to bring the Gae Bulg. He throws the spear at Ferdiad, piercing his armour. Ferdiad dies soon afterwards.

Cu Chulainn throws his magical spear, the Gae Bulg, in his fight against Ferdiad.

Ruyi Jingu Bang

In Chinese mythology, Ruyi Jingu Bang is the name of the magical weapon belonging to the mythical Sun Wukong, the Monkey King. Sun Wukong took it from the underwater palace of the Dragon King. Said to be an immensely heavy iron rod, Sun Wukong can shrink it or make it grow as he wishes. When the rod is not in use, Sun Wukong shrinks it to the size of a sewing needle and keeps it behind his ear.

Magic bows

The archer, Arash, is a heroic figure from Persian myth. In a war between the Persians and their enemies from Central Asia, Arash fires an arrow to decide the boundary between their two lands. The bow he uses has been made by an angel, and fires an arrow that travels from dawn to dusk, and covers a great distance.

A statue of Arash the archer in Tehran, Iran

Gandiva is the name of a magical bow, given to the hero, Arjuna (see pages 36-37) by Agni, god of fire. It is said that Arjuna is given the bow to prevent Indra, god of rain, from putting out Agni's fire. Among Gandiva's many powers is its ability to shoot arrows with extraordinary speed and accuracy, a skill that Arjuna put to good use in the Kurukshetra War.

Sun Wukong, the Monkey King, holds the Ruyi Jingu Bang.

Magical armour

In Hindu mythology, Karna, the son of the Sun God, is a brave and daring warrior. He is born wearing a suit of golden armour that makes him immortal. However, Indra, king of the gods, tricks Karna into giving his armour away. This means that Arjuna is able to kill him with an arrow in the Kurukshetra War (see pages 36-37).

Norse heroes Orvar-Oddr and Beowulf both wear magical shirts that protect them in battle. Orvar-Oddr has a silk coat of mail that no sword nor arrow can pierce. Beowulf has a chainmail coat, made for him by Wayland, the legendary smith. In British legend, Sir Lancelot (see page 17) receives a magical shield from the Lady of the Lake which gives him the strength of three men and stops him feeling tired.

Greek myth has many examples of magical armour. In the Trojan War, Achilles lends his armour to Patroclus and it is later seized by the Trojans. Hephaestus, smith to the gods, makes Achilles some more, including a mighty shield. When Achilles is killed by Paris, Ajax and Odysseus argue about who should inherit his armour. Agamemnon decides to give it to Odysseus and Ajax kills himself in shame.

This painting shows the Norse hero, Orvar-Oddr, and his close friend, the warrior Hjalmar, when Hjalmar lies mortally wounded.

The helmet of Hades

Invisibility

Being able to come and go without being seen is a useful trick for heroes. Various magical items of clothing make this possible. Wearing the helmet of Hades, the Greek hero, Perseus (see page 28), is able to escape unharmed after killing the gorgon, Medusa. In Welsh mythology, the mantle of Arthur is a cloak that enables the wearer to see everything whilst never being seen. The Tarnkappe is another magical cloak, belonging to the hero, Sigurd, that makes its wearer invisible.

Magical vehicles

Magical vehicles often appear in a hero's quest. The Argo, the ship of the Argonauts (see page 8), is said to have been built with the help of the gods. Its bow is made from a magical piece of timber and has the power of prophecy. Gluskab is a hero of Native American myth. He has a magical canoe that is able to grow big enough to carry an army or shrink to fit into the hand.

Thetis dips Achilles into the
River Styx to make him invulnerable.

A hero can become almost impossible to defeat if he has the gift of invulnerability. In many cases, this means bathing, or being dipped, in a liquid that has magical powers. There is always one spot, however, that the magic does not touch and this weak spot almost inevitably leads to the hero's downfall.

When Achilles is born his mother, Thetis, tries to make him immortal by dipping him into the River Styx. When doing this she holds him by his heel so his heel is the only part of his body that does not become invulnerable to attack. Achilles grows up to become a great warrior, fighting bravely in the Trojan War, but he is later killed by an arrow in his heel (see page 34). The term 'Achilles' heel' is still used to describe a person's weak spot.

Esfandyar is a hero from Persian mythology. He is best known for his battle with the great warrior, Rostam (see page 14). Esfandyar is the son of a king who sends him on many missions to put down rebellions and invasions. One day he orders Esfandyar to go and capture Rostam, and to bring him home in chains for not showing respect to the king. Esfandyar challenges Rostam to a fight but, while Rostam is badly wounded, Esfandyar is unhurt. During a break in the fighting, Rostam learns Esfandyar's secret – he has swum in the pool of invincibility and so he cannot be harmed. While he swam, however, he kept his eyes closed. When battle begins again Rostam shoots Esfandyar through the eyes – his only weak point – with a double-headed arrow.

The story of Sigurd and Fafnir (see page 24) is a good example of a hero's quest for invulnerability. After killing Fafnir, the god, Odin, tells Sigurd to drain the dragon's blood and bathe in it. This will make him invulnerable. Sigurd does as Odin says and becomes invincible. Only one part of his body is not affected – one of his shoulders, where a leaf has stuck.

After killing Fafnir, the dragon, Sigurd
bathes in its blood to become
invincible.

Ravana

The great Hindu epic poem, the Ramayana, tells the story of Lord Rama and his quest to rescue his wife, Sita, who has been kidnapped by Ravana. Ravana is usually depicted as an evil demon king but there are stories which praise his great strength. In his youth, he performs a long penance to Lord Brahma, the god of creation. Brahma is pleased with Ravana's devotion and grants him a boon (promise). Ravana asks to become invulnerable but, in his arrogance, he only asks for invulnerability from attacks by the gods or demons. He does not think it worthwhile to ask for protection from mortal men or animals. Ravana is also given the ability to change his shape, and, in the Ramayana, is described as having ten monstrous heads and 20 arms.

The Ramayana tells how Rama and Sita are exiled to the forest. While Rama is out hunting, Ravana appears at Sita's hut. Posing as a poor beggar, he kidnaps Sita and carries her off to his home on the island of Lanka. Lord Rama calls on an army of bears and monkeys to help him rescue Sita and bring her home. When the army reaches Lanka, a terrible battle breaks out, during which Rama kills Ravana. Although Rama is an incarnation of the god, Vishnu, he has been sent down to Earth as a mortal and so is able to pierce Ravana's invulnerability.

Ravana kidnaps Sita and kills Jayatu, the vulture king, in a scene from the Ramayana.

Fong Sai-Yuk

The folk hero, Fong Sai-Yuk, is a character from Chinese legend. His father is a rich businessman, while his mother is a legendary teacher who trains her son in martial arts. Soon he becomes a great fighter. A story tells of how, shortly after Fong Sai-Yuk is born, his mother breaks every bone in his body. Once a bone is broken and mends, it becomes stronger and less breakable. It is said that this gave Fong Sai-Yuk bones of metal and skin of copper. She then bathes him in a special ointment made from herbs which makes him largely invulnerable.

Fong Sai-Yuk goes on to have many adventures, displaying both his extraordinary martial arts skill and his gift of invulnerability. There are several different versions of his death. One tells how he is killed by a notorious martial arts warrior, Bak Mei, in a battle of revenge. Another tells how he dies during a fight with Wu Mei whilst a fire rages around them, destroying the Shaolin temple.

Fong Sai-Yuk's mother breaks his bones before bathing him in a potion that makes him invulnerable.

Glossary

Avenged
Inflicted a punishment in return for harm done to another person.

Banished
Sent away from a place as a punishment.

Birthright
The possessions or position a person is said to be entitled to at birth.

Constellation
A group of stars.

Cyclops
A one-eyed giant from Ancient Greek mythology.

Descendants
People who are descended from earlier members of their family.

Elixir
A magical potion said to be able to give the gift of eternal life.

Epic
Something that is done on a heroic or grand scale. Also a long poem, telling the deeds of a legendary hero.

Executed
Put to death.

Exiled
When a person is sent away from their home country for a long time.

Folklore
The traditional stories and legends of a people or culture that sum up their beliefs and often describe events that happened in their past.

Hero
In Ancient Greek mythology, a hero was a being of amazing courage and strength who was often half-mortal, half-god.

Immortality
Never dying but having everlasting life.

Incarnation
The form a god or goddess takes when he or she appears on earth.

Invulnerable
Unable to be wounded, hurt or damaged.

Knight-errant
A knight who wanders in search of daring and heroic quests.

Legendary
Relating to legends. Legends are traditional stories which are often based on supposedly historical events.

Lyre
A stringed musical instrument from Ancient Greece. It was made from a tortoise shell.

Medieval
Relating to the Middle Ages, a period of European history which lasted from around the 5th century to the 15th century AD.

Mythical
Related to myths. Myths are traditional stories, not based in historical fact but using supernatural characters to explain human behaviour and natural events.

Navigate
To find the way, usually by boat.

Oracle
A shrine in Ancient Greece where people went to consult a priestess who was thought to be able to communicate with the gods.

Outlaw
A person who is not protected by the law and who is forced to live in hiding.

Pagans
A group of people who do not follow a religion.

Penance
A punishment that a person takes on to make up for something they have done wrong.

Pilgrimage
A journey made to a shrine or another sacred place.

Prophecy
A prediction of what will happen in the future.

Pyre
A pile of wood used for cremating (burning) a dead body.

Quest
An expedition by a hero or knight to perform a task, such as finding the Holy Grail.

Rakshasha
A demon in Hindu mythology.

Reconciled
When two people become friends again after a quarrel.

Saga
A long story from Scandinavia, telling of the adventures of heroes or families.

Supernatural
Magical beings, such as fairies, ghosts and gods, and events that cannot be explained by physical or scientific laws.

Index